Everett T. (Everett Titsworth) Tomlinson

A mManual for the Study of Latin Grammar

Everett T. (Everett Titsworth) Tomlinson

A mManual for the Study of Latin Grammar

ISBN/EAN: 9783743394254

Manufactured in Europe, USA, Canada, Australia, Japa

Cover: Foto ©Paul-Georg Meister /pixelio.de

Manufactured and distributed by brebook publishing software
(www.brebook.com)

Everett T. (Everett Titsworth) Tomlinson

A mManual for the Study of Latin Grammar

A

MANUAL

FOR THE

STUDY OF LATIN GRAMMAR.

BY

E. T. TOMLINSON,
HEAD MASTER OF RUTGERS COLLEGE GRAMMAR SCHOOL.

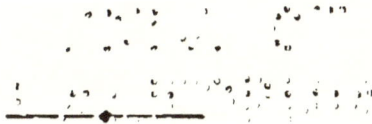

BOSTON:

PUBLISHED BY GINN, HEATH, & CO.

1885.

PREFATORY NOTE.

———•◦•———

I HAVE prepared this little book because of a want I have felt in my own classes. In the usual method of studying the Grammar by reference, the pupils learn separate and distinct fragments, which, if they remain in their minds, are held as units and not as the parts of one whole. For example, they learn at one time that the " Dative Case is used with *esse* to denote the possessor "; and again, that the " Genitive Case is used to denote possession "; and again, that the " Possessive Adjective expresses possession." I have tried to group principles together; and by asking the question, " How is Possession expressed ? " and giving all the references bearing upon that point, to partially arrange their knowledge, and to give some definite aim and end to their study. Without adhering too closely to a rigid system, I have had the synthetic method before me in all the work.

I would here acknowledge the aid I have received from the teachers who have kindly assisted me by their suggestions and criticisms.

E. T. TOMLINSON.

RUTGERS COLLEGE GRAMMAR SCHOOL,
   NEW BRUNSWICK, N.J.
     Jan. 1, 1884.

PREFACE TO THE REVISED EDITION.

TEACHERS have frequently written and have inquired the way in which I advise my little book to be used.

As classes vary in their composition and demands, no fixed rule can be made; but in my own classes I use it, by placing a copy in the hands of each pupil studying Latin, and assigning lessons daily in connection with the regular class work. With certain classes we take only sections, but with the advanced classes we study the book entire.

I have been pleased at the reception the Manual has met.

E. T. TOMLINSON.

RUTGERS COLLEGE GRAMMAR SCHOOL,
Jan. 1, 1885.

EXPLANATION OF REFERENCES AND ABBREVIATIONS.

"A. & G." refers to the Latin Grammar of Allen & Greenough; "H." to Harkness's Latin Grammar; "C. & S." to the Latin Grammar of Chase & Stuart; "N." denotes note; and "re." remark.

In some cases the references given will be found not to contain a direct answer to the question propounded, but they will give the information called for.

A MANUAL FOR THE STUDY OF LATIN GRAMMAR.

QUANTITY AND ACCENT.

1. When is a *syllable or vowel short?*
   A. & G. 18, *a*.   H. 16, 2, ii.   C. & S. 7, 3.

2. When can a *vowel naturally short* be regarded as *long?*
   A. & G. 18, *e*.   C. & S. 7, 1, Ex. 1.

3. What is the *quantity* of a *diphthong?*
   A. & G. 18, *b*.   H. 16, iii. N. 4.   C. & S. 7, 2.

4. In what other cases is a syllable *long in quantity?*
   A. & G. 18, *c, d, e*.

5. What is the rule for *accent?*
   Ans. Generally accent the penult if it is long in quantity; otherwise, accent the antepenult.
   A. & G. 19, *a, b, c*.   H. 17, 18.   C. & S. 9, 10, 11.

INFLECTION.

1. What does *Inflection* include?

2. In *Inflection*, what part of the word remains unchanged?
   A. & G. 21.   H. 46.   C. & S. 15.

3. What is the difference between the *stem* and the *root?*
   A. & G. 21, 22, 23.   H. 313, 314.   C. & S. 15, 16.

4. What parts of speech are *inflected?*

5. What names are considered as *Masculine in Gender?* As *Feminine?* As *Neuter?* Select illustrations of each.
   A. & G. 29.   H. 42, i. 1, 2; ii. 1, 2.   C. & S. 13, i. 1, 2, 3; ii. 1, 2, 3.

NOUNS.

1. What *cases* in the *declension of nouns* have the *same terminations ?*
A. & G. 33, *a, b, e.*   H. 46, 2, 1), 2), 3).   C. & S. 17, 1, 2, 3.

2. Of what *gender* are most *nouns of the First Declension ?*
A. & G. 35.   H. 48.   C. & S. 19.

3. Of what *gender* are the *nouns of the Second Declension ?* State
the endings of each *gender.* A. & G. 39.   H. 51.   C. & S. 21.

4. What are the *terminations* in the *Nominative Singular* of the
Masculine nouns of the Third Declension ?
A. & G. 65, *a.*   H. 99.   C. & S. 30, 1, 4, 7, 9, 10, 13, 15, 16.

5. What are the *terminations* in the *Nominative Singular* of the
Feminine Nouns of the Third Declension ?
A. & G. 65, *b.*   H. 105.   C. & S. 30, 2, 3, 5, 6, 7, 8, 11, 12.

6. What are the *terminations* of the *Neuter nouns* in the *Nominative Singular* of the *Third Declension ?*
A. &. G. 65, *c.*   H. 111.   C. & S. 30, 14, 15.

7. What is the *gender* of the *nouns of the Third Declension* with
the following *terminations in the Nominative Singular ? —*
a, or, ās, gs, l, men, ur, ūs, ŭs, ēs, ĕs.
A. & G. 65, *a, b, c.*   H. 99–115.   C. & S. 30, 1–16.

8. How is the *Nominative Singular* of the *First Declension* formed ?
A. & G. 34, N.   H. 48, foot-note 3.

9. How is the *Nominative Singular* of the *Second Declension*
formed ?   A. & G. 37, N.   H. 51, 1, 2).   C. & S. 21, 1, 2.

10. What is the difference in the formation of the *Nominative Singular* between *ager* and *puer ?*
A. & G. 38, 42.   H. 51, 1, 4), 5).

11. How are nouns of the *Third Declension* classified according
to their *stem endings ?*
A. & G. 43, N.   H. 56, i., ii.   C. & S. 26, 1, 2.

12. Mention the *Mutes* and their divisions.   Mention the *Liquids.*

13. How do *Masculine and Feminine nouns of the Third Declension,* *with stems ending in a Mute,* form their *Nominative Singular?* How do *Neuter nouns?*

      A. & G. 44. H. 67. C. & S. 29,. i.

14. How is the *Nominative Singular of stems ending in a Liquid* of the *Third Declension* formed?

     A. & G. 48, *a, b, c, d, e.* H. 60, 1, 3). C. & S. 29, i.

15. What peculiarities in declension have the *vowel* or *i-stems* of the Third Declension ?

      A. & G. 55, *a, b, c, d, e.* H. 62–65.
      C. & S. 29, v., vi., vii., ix., 1–8, xi.

16. In what *nouns of the Third Declension* can *ium* be found in the *Genitive Plural?*
 See A. & G. Latin Method. A. & G. 55, *a,* 53, *a, b,* 54, 1, 2, 3.
      H. 65, 1, 2, 3. C. & S. 29, ix. 1–8.

17. Form the Nominative Singular from the following stems : *stella, domino, puer, dent, leon, corpor, animal, duc, milit. capit, patr.* Explain the process.

18. What is peculiar in the declension of *filia, filius, deus, Vergilius, sol, pelagus ?*

19. Name three *irregularly neuter nouns of the Second Declension.*
     A. & G. 39, *b.* H. 51, 7. C. & S. 23, 7.

20. Decline *vis, senex, bos, dea, Aeneas, Delos.*

21. What *nouns of the Fourth Declension* have the ending *-ubus* in the *Dative* and *Ablative Plural?*
     A. & G. 70, *d.* H. 117, 1, 1), 2), 3). C. & S. 34, 4.

22. Of what *gender* are most *nouns of the Fourth Declension ?*
     A. & G. 69, *a, b.* H. 116, 118. C. & S. 34, 5.

23. How do *nouns of the Fourth Declension* form their *Nominative Singular?*   A. & G. 67, N.

24. What *nouns of the Fifth Declension* have any forms of the *plural,* and *what nouns are masculine?*
     A. & G. 73, 74, *d.* H. 122, 1, 2, 120. C. & S. 35, 1, 5.

25. Decline *domus, cantus, manus, dies, res.*

26. What is an *Epicene noun?*
          A. & G. 30, *b.*   H. 43, 3.   C. & S. 13, i. 3.

27. What are *Heteroclitic and Heterogeneous nouns?*
          A. & G. 78, 79.   H. 127, iii., iv.   C. & S. 37, 6, 7.

28. What peculiarities are there in the declension of *Proper nouns?*
          A. & G. 40, *c.*   H. 130, 2.   C. & S. 37, 2, *a.*

29. What are the *Indirect or Oblique cases?*
          A. & G. 31, N.   C. & S. 14, 3.

30. What *Adjectives* are or can be used as *nouns?*
          A. & G. 88, *a,* 86, *c,* 94, *e.*   H. 441.   C. & S. 113, 7, 8.

31. What *forms of the verb* are or can be used as *nouns?*
          A. & G. 114, *a, b,* 112, *d.*   H. 200, i., ii., iii., iv.
                                  C. & S. 65, 3, 4, 5, 6.

32. In what *case* is the *subject of a sentence?*
          A. & G. 173, also note.   H. 368, 536.   C. & S. 109, 1, 3.

33. By what *cases* can the *object of a verb be expressed?*
          A. & G. 237, 219, 221, *a, b, c,* 222, 227, 249.
          H. 371, 407, 406, i., ii., iii., 385, i., ii., 421, i., ii.
C. & S. 121, 137, also Ex., 138, 139, 1, 2, 142, 1, 2, 3, 153, 167, i., 168.

34. By what *case* is the *Indirect Object* expressed?
          A. & G. 224.   H. 382, 384, i., ii.   C. & S. 108, 6.

35. In what ways can *possession* be expressed?
          A. & G. 214, 214, *a,* 231.   H. 396, i., 401, N. 3, 387.
                         C. & S. 133, 1, N. 2, 156.

36. What is the distinction in Question 35 between the use of the *Genitive* and *Dative?*   A. & G. 231, remark.

37. How can *Agency* be expressed?
          A. & G. 246, *b,* 232, *a, b,* 263.   H. 388, 2, 415, i. 1, N. 1.
                         C. & S. 157, 173, 1, 2.

38. What is the *Partitive Genitive?*
          A. & G. 216.   H. 397.   C. & S. 133, 4.

39. In what manner is the *idea of the Partitive Genitive* sometimes expressed?   A. & G. 216, *c.*   C. & S. 133, 4, N. 4, N. 5.

40. How is the *material of which* anythiug is composed expressed?
A. & G. 244, 214, *e.*   H. 415, iii.   C. & S. 172, 133, 6.

41. How is the *place to which* expressed?
A. & G. 257, *b*, 258, *b.*   H. 380, i., ii., 1, 2.   C. & S. 129, 1, 130, 1, 2, 3.

42. How is the *place from which* expressed?
A. & G. 243, *c*, 258, *a.*   H. 412, i., ii.   C. & S. 182, 1, 2.

43. How is the *place at which* or *where* expressed?
A. & G. 258, *c, d, e, f.*   H. 425, i., ii.   C. & S. 183, 1, 148, 1, 2.

44. How is *duration of time* or *time how long* expressed?
A. & G. 256.   H. 379.   C. & S. 129, 1, 2.

45. How is *time at which* or *time when* expressed?
A. & G. 256.   H. 429.   C. & S. 185.

46. How is *time within which* expressed?
A. & G. 256.   H. 430.   C. & S. 185.

47. What cases express *source?*
A. & G. 214, *e*, 244.   H. 413, 415.   C. & S. 178.

48. What constructions denoting *source* are used with *participles denoting birth or origin?*
A. & G. 244, *a.*   H. 415, ii.   C. & S. 178, 1.

49. What cases express *quality?*
A. & G. 215, 251.   H. 419, ii.   C. & S. 175, 134.

50. What distinction is to be made between the different cases used in Question 49?   A. & G. 251, *a.*   C. & S. 134, N. 1.

51. What cases are used to *complete the meaning of Adjectives?*
A. & G. 218, 234, 247.   H. 399, 391, 417.
C. & S. 136, 162, 181, 174.

52. How is *price or value* expressed?
A. & G. 252, 215, *c.*   H. 422, 404, 405.
C. & S. 179, 146, 147, 1, 2.

53. How is *specification* or *that in respect to which a statement is modified* expressed?
A. & G. 253, 240, *b, c.*   H. 424, 378.   C. & S. 180, 123, 1.

54. What is the *Cognate Accusative?*
      A. & G. 238.   H. 371, i. 1).   C. & S. 123.

55. How is the *degree of difference* expressed?
      A. & G. 250.   H. 423.   C. & S. 176.

56. How are *means, manner,* and *instrument* expressed?
      A. & G. 248.   H. 418, 419, iii.   C. & S. 166, 1, 2, 3.

57. How is *accompaniment* expressed ?
      A. & G. 248, *a.*   H. 419, i.   C. & S. 166, 5.

58. When can *cum* be omitted in the construction of Question 57?
      A. & G. 248, *a.*

59. What *English idiom or expression* does the *Ablative Absolute* often resemble? — *Ans.* The Parenthesis.

60. What words are used in the construction called the *Ablative Absolute?* How are they used?
      A. & G. 255, *a.*   H. 431, 1, 2.   C. & S. 187, 1, 2, 3.

61. What *Prepositions* are used with the *Accusative?*
      A. & G. 152, *a.*   H. 433.   C. & S. 131, 1.

62. What *Prepositions* are used with the *Ablative?*
      A. & G. 152, *b.*   H. 434.   C. & S. 186.

63. What *Prepositions* are used with *either the Accusative or Ablative?*   A. & G. 152, *c.*   H. 435.   C. & S. 131, 3.

64. What is the distinction in the use of *in* and *sub* with the *Accusative* and with the *Ablative?*
      A. & G. 152, *c.*   H. 435, i.   C. & S. 131, 3.

65. What *verbs* govern *two Accusatives?*
      A. & G. 239, *a, b, c, d.*   H. 373, 374, 375, 376.
      C. & S. 122, N. 2, 124, N. 2, 126, 127.

66. What *prepositions in composition with verbs* govern the *Dative?*
      A. & G. 228.   H. 386.   C. & S. 154.

67. What cases and constructions require *prepositions*, and in what can the *Preposition* be omitted?

68. What construction is used with *verbs of accusing*, etc.?
      A. & G. 220.   H. 409, ii.   C. & S. 140.

69. What is the *Dative of Reference?*
 A. & G. 235. H. 382, 384, ii. 4. C. & S., 158.

70. What case follows *nouns of action, agency, and feeling?*
 A. & G. 217. H. 395, 396, iii. C. & S. 133, 2, 3.

71. What case or cases are used in *exclamations?*
 A. & G. 240, *d*, 241. H. 381, 369. C. & S. 120, 2, 3, 132.

72. What is the distinction in the use of the *Genitive and Dative with similis?*
 A. & G. 234, *d*, remark. H. 391, foot-notes 1 and 3. C. & S. 162, 4.

73. What cases are used with *causa, erga, propius, instar, prope, proximus?*

74. What case follows the *comparative degree* when *quam is not expressed?* What case when *quam* is expressed?
 A. & G. 247, *a*. H. 417, 1. C. & S. 174.

75. How were the following expressions stated in Latin? *at home; on the ground; at Athens; at Cures; at Carthage.*
 A. & G. 258, *c*. H. 48, 4, 51, 8. C. & S. 19, 5, 23, 8.

76. When does *ad with the Accusative* have the meaning of *near?*
 A. & G. 259, *f*. H. 433, i., 446, N. 4. C. & S. 183, 6, *a*.

77. What prepositions express the relations of *to, in, from, at?*
 A. & G. 259, *f*. H. 433, i., 434, i. C. & S. 183, 1, 6, *a*, 131, 3.

78. When is the preposition *super* used with the *Accusative* and when with the *Ablative?*
 A. & G. 260, *c*. H. 435, i. C. & S. 131, 4.

79. What constructions follow *verbs of plenty and want?*
 A. & G. 223, 243. H. 421, ii., 399, 3. C. & S. 170, 143.

80. What case is used with *opus* and *usus?*
 A. & G. 243, *e*. H. 414, iv. C. & S. 171.

81. What case is used with *miseret?*
 A. & G. 221, *b*. H. 409, iii. C. & S. 139, 2.

82. What other verbs are used similarly to *miseret?*
 A. & G. 221, *b*. H. 409, iii. C. & S. 139, 2.

83. What distinction, if any, is made between the *Ablative* and *Genitive of Quality ?*
> A. & G. 215, N.   H. 419, iii. 2.   C. & S. 134, N. I.

84. In a tabular form arrange the leading uses of each case.

85. Arrange in a tabular form the particulars wherein the cases resemble one another; as, " The Gen. and Abl. are used to express quality"; "The Dative and Ablative are used to express agency," etc.

86. Arrange in a tabular form the particulars wherein the cases are opposed to one another; as, " The Acc. is used to express motion to, the Abl. motion from a place," etc.

VERBS.

1. What are the *tenses of the verb*, and what time does each denote?   A. & G. 115.   H. 197.   C. & S. 66, 1, 2, 3, 4, 5, 6.

2. Into what *two classes* are these divided?
> A. & G. 108, *c*, 285, 1, 2.   H. 198.   C. & S. 66, 7.

3. What point in common have the *Present* and *Imperfect Tenses ?*
> A. & G. 115, *a*, 2.   H. 467, ii., 469, ii.   C. & S. 66, 1, 3.

4. What two uses has the *Perfect Tense ?*
> A. & G. 115, *c*.   H. 471, i. ii.   C. & S. 66, 4.

5. What is the distinction as regards time between the *Perfect* and *Imperfect Tenses ?*
> A. & G. 115, *b*.   H. 471, i., ii., 469, i., ii.   C. & S. 66, 3, 4.

6. What are the *personal and tense endings, Active and Passive ?*
> A. & G. 118.   H. 242, 243, 247, 248.   C. & S. 91, 92.

7. What is the rule for the *sequence of tenses ?*
> A. & G. 286.   H. 491.   C. & S. 234.

8. What *tenses has the Subjunctive ?*
> A. & G. 110, *a*.   H. 197, ii., N. 2, 478.

9. What is the distinction in the use of the *Active and Passive Voices ?*   A. & G. 111.   H. 195, i., ii.   C. & S. 64.

10. What peculiar use does the *Passive Voice* often have?
> A. & G. 111, *b*, N. I.   H. 465.   C. & S. 64, 2.

11. What class of verbs is used only in the *Passive form* with the *Active or Reflexive meaning?*

        A. & G. 111, 2.   H. 195, ii. 2.   C. & S. 64, 1.

12. How are the different *persons* and *numbers* expressed?

        A. & G. 108, 2, *d.*   H. 199, N.   C. & S. 89, 1.

13. Name the *conjugations* and the distinctive features of each.

        A. & G. 122, 126, *a, b, c, d.*   H. 201.   C. & S. 73.

14. Define the term *principal parts*, and name each.

        A. & G. 122, *b, c.*   H. 202, 220.   C. & S. 69.

15. Which conjugations are *primitive* and which *causative?*

        A. & G. 165.

16. In the derivative verbs, what are the *inceptive* or *inchoative endings*, and what do they signify?

        A. & G. 167, *a.*   H. 337, 281.   C. & S. 88, 1.

17. The *frequentative, intensive,* or *iterative* endings?

        A. & G. 167, *b, c.*   H. 336, i., ii.   C. & S. 88, 2.

18. The *diminutives?*   A. & G. 167, *d.*   H. 339.   C. & S. 88, 5.

19. The *desideratives?*   A. & G. 167, *e.*   II. 338.   C. & S. 88, 4.

20. What is the force of the *preposition* in *compound verbs?*

A. & G. 170, *a, b,* 120, *a, b.*   H. 344, foot-note 2.   C. & S. 101, i.

21. How many and what *stems* has a *transitive verb?*

        A. & G. 121.   H. 251, 252, 256.   C. & S. 68, 1, 2, 3.

22. How is the *present stem* formed and found?

        A. & G. 123, *a, b, c, d, e.*   H. 251, 1–6.   C. & S. 94, i., ii.

23. What forms of the verb are made from the *present stem?*

Ans. The *Present, Imperfect, and Future Indicative, Active and Passive; Present and Imperfect Subjunctive, Active and Passive;* the *Present and Future Imperative, Active and Passive; Present Infinitive, Active and Passive; Present Active Participle; Future Passive Participle (Gerundive);* and the *Gerund.*

Learn thoroughly, and give synopses by the different persons and numbers of the entire present system.

A thorough knowledge of *sum* is pre-supposed.

24. How is the *Perfect stem* formed and found?
    A. & G. 124, *a*, *b*, *c*, *d*, *e*.   H. 252, 253, 254, 255.   C. & S. 95, 1–6.

25. What forms of the verb are made from the *Perfect stem ?*
    Ans. The *Perfect, Pluperfect,* and *Future Perfect Indicative Active;* the *Perfect and Pluperfect Subjunctive Active,* and the *Perfect Infinitive Active.*

26. How is the *Supine stem* formed and found?
    A. & G. 125, *a*, *b*.   H. 256, 1.   C. & S. 96.

27. What forms of the verb are made from the *Supine stem?*
    Ans. The *Future Infinitive Active ;* the *Future and Perfect Infinitive Passive; Future Participle, Active ; Perfect Participle ; Accusative and Ablative of the Supine ; Perfect, Pluperfect, and Future Perfect Indicative Passive;* and the *Perfect and Pluperfect Subjunctive Passive.*

The teacher should insist, in the early study of the language especially, upon rapid and accurate synopses of the verb in each person and number, by moods and voices, and upon the conjugation of tenses and statement of comparative forms.

The perception of differences is, or should be, most fully developed in the study of language.   The pupil, with careful practice, will soon gain such proficiency that the form will instantly suggest its location, meaning, and use.

28. What is the general use of the *Indicative mood?*
    A. & G. 112, *a*, 264.   H. 474.   C. & S. 65, 188.

29. What *forms of the indicative* sometimes have the use of the *Imperative?* A. & G. 269, *f.* H. 487, 4. C. & S. 191, 2, 247, 3, 5.

30. What use has the *Indicative* in *Causal Sentences?*
    A. & G. 321, 333.   H. 516, i.   C. & S. 224, N. 2, 232.

31. What take the place of the *Future Indicative* in *Indirect Discourse?* A. & G. 334, *a.*   H. 529, ii. 4.   C. & S. 234, 7.

32. When is the *Indicative* used in *Subordinate Clauses* in *Indirect Discourse?*   A. & G. 336, *b.*   H. 524, 2.   C. & S. 228, 5.

33. What forms of *Present and Past Conditional Sentences* require the *Indicative?*
    A. & G. 306, 308, *b, c.*   H. 508.   C. & S. 188, 1, 215, 2.

34. What forms of *Future Conditional Sentences* require the *Indicative?* A. & G. 307, *a*. H. 508. C. & S. 215, 2.

35. When is the *Indicative* used in *General Conditions?* A. & G. 309, *c*. H. 508, 5. C. & S. 215, 2, 3.

36. What special use has the *Indicative of verbs signifying necessity, propriety,* and the like? A. & G. 311, *c*. H. 511, 1, N. 3.

Synopses of the Indicative mood of many different verbs in each person and number, with the equivalents of each form in English, should be frequently required.

37. How is a *present condition, in which nothing is implied as to the truth of the statement,* expressed? A. & G. 306. H. 508. C. & S. 215, 2.

38. How is a *present condition, in which the condition is not fulfilled,* expressed? A. & G. 308. H. 510. C. & S. 215, 4.

39. How is the *more vivid future condition* expressed? A. & G. 307. H. 508. C. & S. 215, 2.

40. The *less vivid future condition* is how expressed? A. & G. 307. H. 509. C. & S. 215, 3.

41. How is a *past conditional statement, in which nothing is implied as to the truth of the statement,* expressed? A. & G. 306. H. 508. C. & S. 215, 2.

42. How is a *past condition, in which the condition was not fulfilled,* expressed? A. & G. 308. H. 510. C. & S. 215, 4.

43. What is the rule for the statement of general conditions? A. & G. 309, *a, b, c*. H. 508, 5, 1), 2).

44. Is the *conditional part of the sentence* ever omitted?, A. & G. 310, *a, b, c,* 311. H. 549, 2. C. & S. 219.

45. Mention the *particles* used in introducing *conditional sentences*. A. & G. 304, *a*, N. H. 311, 3, 513, i., ii. C. & S. 215, 1, N. 2.

46. What is the distinction between the *time expressed* by the *Indicative and Subjunctive moods?* A. & G. 264, *a*, 323. H. 478. C. & S. 214.

47. What constructions are used with *cum temporal?* When is each used? A. & G. 325. H. 521, i., ii. 1, 2. C. & S. 214, 4, 5.

48. What *other temporal particles* are used in the same construction in which *cum* is?
A. & G. 327. H. 519, ii. 520, i. 1, 2, ii. C. & S. 214, 1, 2.

49. What are the *common adverbs of time*, and with what *moods* are they used?
A. & G. 149, *b*, 324, 322, 328, re. H. 519, 520.
C. & S. 193, 1, 214, 1, 2, 3.

50. What are the uses of the *Independent Subjunctive?*
A. & G. 265, *a*. H. 483, 1, 2, 4, 484, i., ii., iii., iv. C. & S. 201, i.

51. What are the uses of the *Subjunctive in Dependent clauses?*
A. & G. 265, *b*. H. 497, 498, 500, 504. C. & S. 201, ii.

52. What is the general rule for the *expression of a wish?*
A. & G. 267. H. 483. C. & S. 203, 1, 2, 3.

53. What is the *distinction in tense* in the uses in Question 52?
A. & G. 267. H. 483, 2. C. & S. 203, 2

54. What *particles* are common in the use in Question 52?
A. & G. 267, *b*. H. 483, 1. C. & S. 203, 2, 3.

55. What special uses have *velim, vellem, and their compounds?*
A. & G. 267, *c*. C. & S. 202, 2, N.

56. What special use has the *Future Indicative in place of the Imperative?* A. & G. 269, *d*. H. 487, 4. C. & S. 247, 3, 5.

57. What *forms of the Subjunctive* are used to denote a *mild form of command?* A. & G. 266. H. 483, 2. C. & S. 203, 2, 8.

58. How is a *strong command* expressed?
A. & G. 269. H. 487. C. & S. 65, 2.

59. What are the common constructions in *prohibitions?*
A. & G. 266, *a*, 269, *a*. H. 484, iv. N. 1, N. 2, 487, 1, 2).
C. & S. 203, 5, 7, 247, 5, N. 1.

60. How are *simple questions* introduced?
A. & G. 210, *a, b, c, d, e, f*. H. 351, 1, N. 1, N. 2, N. 3, N. 4, 2, 3, 4.
C. & S. 258, 1, 2, 3, 5.

61. How are *double questions* introduced?
A. & G. 211, *a, b, c, d.* H. 353, 1, 2.
C. & S. 258, 6, 7, 8, 10, 11, 12, 13.

62. In what kind of questions is the *Indicative mood* used?
A. & G. 264. H. 196, i. C. & S. 188.

63. In what kind of questions is the *Subjunctive mood* used?
A. & G. 268, 334. H. 529, i. C. & S. 231, 1.

64. What is the most common manner of expressing *purpose*?
A. & G. 317, 318, *a.* H. 497, i., ii. C. & S. 201, 1.

65. In how many and what ways may *purpose* be expressed?
A. & G. 318. H. 497, i., ii., 533, ii., 542, i. N. 2, 542, iii. N. 2, 544, 2, N. 2, 546, 549, 3. C. & S. 206, 222, 244, 1, 249, 1, 250, 252, 6, 7, 9, 1, 252, 12, 253, N.

66. How is *negative purpose* introduced?
A. & G. 331, 318, *a*, 319, *d*, N., re. H. 497, ii. C. & S. 206, 3, 4.

67. In what construction is the *Supine* used to express *purpose*?
A. & G. 318, 2, *c*, 302. H. 546. C. & S. 253.

68. What is the *Gerundive* use in expressing *purpose*?
A. & G. 318, 2, *b*, 300. H. 544, 2, N. 2. C. & S. 252, 6, 7, 9.

69. How is the *future active participle* used in expressing *purpose*?
A. & G. 318, 2, *d.* H. 549, 3. C. & S. 249, 1, 250.

70. When is the particle *ut* omitted in *clauses of purpose*?
A. & G. 331, *f*, re. H. 502, 1, 2, 499, 2. C. & S. 209, 4, 5.

71. With what verbs is the *Infinitive mood* used to express *purpose*?
A. & G. 331, *a, b, c, d.* H. 533, ii. C. & S. 244, 1.

72. What is the common manner of expressing *result*?
A. & G. 319. H. 500, ii., i. C. & S. 207.

73. How is *negative result* introduced?
A. & G. 319, *d*, N., re. H. 500, ii. C. & S. 207, 203.

74. How are *quin* and *quominus* used in clauses of *result*?
A. & G. 319, *c, d.* H. 504, 4, 500, ii., 501, ii. 2. C. & S. 211, 1.

75. What words besides *ut* sometimes introduce clauses of *result?*
    A. & G. 319, *d*, re.   H. 500, i., ii., 501, ii. 2, iii., 502, 1, 2, 3
    503, i., ii. 1, 2, 3.   C. & S. 207, 208.

76. What is the *Subjunctive of characteristic*, and how is it ex-
    pressed?   A. & G. 320.   H. 503, i.   C. & S. 223, 1.

77. In what special construction is the *Subjunctive of characteristic*
    sometimes used?
    A. & G. 320, *a, b, c, d*.   H. 503, i., foot-note.   C. & S. 223, 1, N. 1.

78. What constructions are used with the temporal particle *cum?*
              A. & G. 325.   H. 521, i., ii. 1, 2.   C. & S. 214, 4, 5.

79. What constructions are used with the causal particle *cum?*
              A. & G. 321, *c*, 326, *a, b*.   H. 517.   C. & S. 214, 3.

80. What particles have a use similar to that of *cum*, in narration?
    A. & G. 327.   H. 520, i. 1, 2, ii., 519, i., ii. 1, 2.   C. & S. 214, 2.

81. What moods (and when) are used with *dum, donec, quoad,
    dummodo?*
    A. & G. 328, 314.   H. 513, i., 519, i., ii. 1, 2.   C. & S. 214, 1.

82. Describe the *Concessive Subjunctive* and the *particles used
    with it.*
    A. & G. 313, 266, *c*.   H. 515, i., ii., iii.   C. & S. 204, 1, 2, 214, 3, 225.

THE INFINITIVE.

1. *The Infinitive* is a form of the verb with what force?
   A. & G. 108, *b*, foot-note 1.   H. 200, i., 532.   C. & S. 235, 65, 3.

2. What are its chief uses?
              A. & G. 112, *d*.   H. 533, 534, 536, 538, 539, i., ii., iii., iv.
              C. & S. 236, 237, 238, 239, 240, 241, 242.

3. Describe the uses of the *Infinitive mood* as the *subject.*
              A. & G. 270.   H. 538, 1, 2, 3.   C. & S. 239, 1, 2, 3.

4. When *used as a verb* in what case is its subject if it has one?
              A. & G. 240, *f*.   H. 536.   C. & S. 109, 3.

5. When the *subject of the Infinitive* is not expressed, in what case is a *predicate noun or adjective after the Infinitive?*
A. & G. 272, *b.* H. 536, 2, 1), 2), 3).

6. Is the *subject of the Infinitive* ever attracted to or expressed in any other case than the *Accusative?*
A. & G. 272, *a*, 275. H. 536, 1. C. & S. 109, 3, Ex.

7. What is the common use of the *Infinitive* with other verbs?
A. & G. 271. H. 533, i. 1, 2. C. & S. 237.

8. What is the use of the *Infinitive in Exclamations?*
A. & G. 274. H. 539, iii. C. & S. 240.

9. In what constructions does the *Infinitive* express *purpose?*
A. & G. 273, *a, b, c, d.* H. 533, ii. N. 2. C. & S. 244, 1.

10. With what parts of speech does the *Infinitive* have the *Greek Accusative* use? A. & G. 273, *d.* H. 533, ii. 3. C. & S. 244, 3.

11. In what tenses is the *Infinitive* used?
A. & G. 288. H. 537. C. & S. 246.

12. What is the *Historical Infinitive?* A. & G. 275. H. 536, 1.

13. What *time* do the *tenses of the Infinitive* express?
A. & G. 288. H. 537. C. & S. 246.

14. How is the *Infinitive* used in *Indirect Discourse?*
A. & G. 336. H. 523, i., ii. 2. C. & S. 228, 1.

15. Describe the uses of the tenses of the Infinitive in Indirect Discourse. A. & G. 288, *b, c, d, e, f.* H. 530, 1). C. & S. 228, 8.

Give examples, orally and in writing, original and selected, from authors, of the principles contained in Question 15.

PARTICIPLES.

1. In what tenses are *participles* found, and with what distinction as regards time? A. & G. 290. H. 550. C. & S. 65, 4, 249.

2. What is used instead of a *present passive participle?*
A. & G. 290, *c.* H. 550, N. 5. C. & S. 249, 2.

3. What peculiar uses has the *present participle?*
A. & G. 290, *a*, 291, 292, *e*, 113, *a.* H. 200, iv., 548. C. & S. 251, 9.

4. What peculiar uses has the *perfect participle?*
    A. & G. 290, *b*, *d*, 291, 292, *c*, *d*, 113, *c*.   H. 200, iv., 548.
                                                    C. & S. 251, 4, 9.

5. What peculiar uses has the *future participle?*
    A. & G. 293, *a*, *b*, *c*, 113, *b*.   H. 549, 3.   C. & S. 249, 1.

6. What are the uses of the *future passive participle?*
    A. & G. 294, *a*, *b*, *c*, *d*, 135, *d*, 113, *d*.   H. 543, 544, 1, 2, notes.
    C. & S. 252, 2, 4, 5, 6, 7, 9, 10, 11, 12, 13, 14, 15, 16, 17.

7. What *participles* do *Deponent Verbs* have?
                        A. & G. 135, *a*.   H. 231, 1.   C. & S. 79.

8. The *participle* is a *form of the verb* having what force?
            A. & G. 113, *e*, *g*.   H. 200, iv., 548.   C. & S. 251, 9.

9. What *participles* have the use of nouns?   When?
                A. & G. 113, *f*.   H. 441, 1, 2, 3.   C. & S. 251, 10.

10. Describe the *uses of the participle* in the *Ablative Absolute*.
    A. & G. 255, *a*, *b*, foot-note.   H. 431, 4, N. 2.   C. & S. 187, 1, 4, 5.

11. What use has the *participle in -urus* with the forms of *fui* in
    conditional sentences?
                A. & G. 308, *d*.   H. 511, 2.   C. & S. 228, 6.

12. What is the common method of *translating the participle* in
    the construction of Question 10?
            A. & G. 255, N.   H. 431, 2.   C. & S. 187, 3.

THE GERUND.

1. What is the force of the *Gerund* and in what *cases* is it found?
    A. & G. 109, *b*, 114, *a*, 295.   H. 200, ii., 542.   C. & S. 65, 5.

2. From what *stem of the verb* is it formed?

3. How does the *Gerund govern* the following word?
                    A. & G. 295.   H. 541.   C. & S. 252.

4. By what are the *Nominative uses of the Gerund* supplied?
                A. & G. 295, re.   C. & S. 252, 14, N. 1.

5. Mention other constructions of the Gerund.
        A. & G. 297, 298, *a*, 301, re.   H. 542, i., ii., iii., iv.
                C. & S. 252, 2, 3, 4, 5, 6, 7, 9, 11, 13.

THE GERUNDIVE.

1. What is the *Gerundive*, and what is its common use?
   A. & G. 109, *a*, foot-note 3.   H. 543.   C. & S. 252, 17.

2. When used *Adjectively*, what is its force in translation?
   A. & G. 113, *d*, 294.   H. 544, 1, 2.
   C. & S. 252, 4, 6, 7, 8, 9, 10, 11, 12, 13, 14, 15, 16, 17.

3. When and how does the *Gerundive* express *purpose?*
   A. & G. 294, *d*, 300.   H. 544, 2, N. 2.   C. & S. 252, 9, 1.

4. What construction is frequently used in place of the *Gerund*
   and a *direct object?*   A. & G. 296.   H. 544, 1.   C. & S. 252, 2.

   Causa videndi Caesarem = *Gerund construction.*
   Causa Caesaris videndi = *Gerundive construction.*

THE SUPINES.

1. How is the *Supine Stem* of the verb formed?
   A. & G. 125, *a, b*.   H. 256, 1, 222, iii. 2, N.   C. & S. 96.

2. What force have the *forms of the Supine?*
   A. & G. 109, *c*.   H. 200, iii.   C. & S. 65, 6.

3. In what *cases* is it found?
   A. & G. 71, *a*, 114, *b*.   H. 200, iii., 545, N. 1.   C. & S. 65, 6.

4. With what *parts of speech* is each used?
   A. & G. 114, *b*.   H. 546, 3, 547, 1.   C. & S. 253, 254.

5. Is the *Supine* parsed as having *person and number?*
   A. & G. 301, N.

6. By what term is the *Supine in -um* sometimes called?
   A. & G. 302.

7. The *Supine in -um* has what use?
   A. & G. 302, 318, *c*.   H. 546, 2, 3.   C. & S. 253, 1, 2, 3, 85, 7, 2.

8. The *Supine in -u* has what use?
   A. & G. 303, re.   H. 547.   C. & S. 254, 1, 2.

9. Does the *Supine* govern as a *verb or noun?*
   A. & G. 303, foot-note 1.   H. 545, N. 1, 547, N.   C. & S. 253, 1.

PRONOUNS.

1. Define and classify *pronouns*.
   A. & G. 25, *c*.   H. 182, foot-note 2, 183, 1, 2, 3, 4, 5, 6.
   C. & S. 57–62.

2. What often takes the place of the *third personal pronoun?*
   A. & G. 98, *b*.   H. 450.   C. & S. 116.

3. What use, in addition to the common one, have the *personal pronouns?*   A. & G. 98, *a*.   H. 448, N.   C. & S. 117.

4. What is the distinction in the use of the two forms of the *genitive plural* of *ego* and *tu?*
   A. & G. 194, *b*.   H. 446, N. 3.   C. & S. 57, 6.

5. When is the *pronoun as subject* expressed?
   A. & G. 194, *a*, 346, *d*.   H. 446.   C. & S. 109, 2.

6. What is the general rule for the construction of *personal pronouns?*   A. & G. 194.   H. 184, foot-note 3.

7. Define the term *demonstrative pronoun*, and decline each.
   A. & G. 100, 101.   H. 186, i., ii., iii., iv., v., vi.   C. & S. 59, i., ii.

8. What case do all the pronouns (except *ipse*) lack?
   A. & G. 101.   H. 184–190.   C. & S. 57–62.

9. What is the distinctive use of *hic, ille, iste*, and *is?*
   A. & G. 102, *a, b, c, d, e*.   H. 450, 1, 2, 3, 4, 451, 1, 2, 3, 4, 5.
   C. & S. 116, 1, 2, 3, 4, 5, 6.

10. What uses has the pronoun *ipse?*
    A. & G. 195, *f, g, h, i, k, l*.   H. 452, 1, 2, 3, 4, 5, 6.   C. & S. 118, 1, 2.

11. What is the rule for the gender of *demonstrative pronouns* when used *adjectively?*
    A. & G. 186, 195, *d*.   H. 438.   C. & S. 113, 1.

12. What use does *idem* often have?
    A. & G. 195, *e*.   H. 451, 3.   C. & S. 116, 7.

13. What is the general rule for the syntax of *demonstrative pronouns?*   A. & G. 195.   H. 438, 1.   C. & S. 113.

14. Decline the *Relative Pronoun*.
    A. & G. 103.   H. 187.   C. & S. 62, 1.

15. How, and with what significations, is the *stem* of the Relative compounded?
A. & G. 105, *a, b, c, d.* H. 190, 191. C. & S. 62, 13, 14, 15.

16. What term is applied to a clause introduced by a *Relative Pronoun?* A. & G. 180, *c.* C. & S. 222, N. 2.

17. What is the rule for the agreement of a *Relative Pronoun?*
A. & G. 198. H. 445. C. & S. 114, 1.

18. Is the *antecedent* always expressed?
A. & G. 200, *c.* H. 445, 6. C. & S. 114, 2, *b.*

19. What exceptions occur in the agreement of a *Relative Pronoun* with its *antecedent* in gender?
A. & G. 199, *b.* H. 445, 2, 3. C. & S. 114, 4.

20. Is the *Relative Pronoun* ever omitted? A. & G. 201, *a.*

21. What pronoun is most frequently used as the *antecedent* of a *Relative Pronoun?* A. & G. 102, *d.* H. 451. C. & S. 116, 6, 6.

22. State the use of the *Relative* in introducing *clauses expressing purpose.* A. & G. 317. H. 497, i. C. & S. 222.

23. State the use of the *Relative* in introducing *result.*
A. & G. 319. H. 500, i. C. & S. 223, 1, 2, 3, 4, 5.

24. What *adjectives* take a *clause expressing result*, with the relative? A. & G. 320, *f.* H. 503, ii. 1, 2, 3. C. & S. 223, 2.

25. Decline the *Interrogative and Indefinite Pronouns.*
A. & G. 104. H. 188, 190. C. & S. 62, 2, 5.

26. State the distinction in form between the *Indefinite and Relative Pronouns.* A. & G. 104, *a.* H. 188. C. & S. 62, 1, 2.

27. How is the *Interrogative form* modified?
A. & G. 105, *b.* H. 188, ii. 3. C. & S. 62, 12, 14, 1–11.

28. State and decline the compounds of the *Interrogative form.*
A. & G. 105, *c, d, i.* H. 188, ii. 3, 190, 1, 2, 1), 2).
C. & S. 62, 14, 1–11.

29. Which is the most definite and which the least so of the *Indefinite Pronouns?* What is the difference in use and meaning between *aliquis* and *quidam?*
A. & G. 202, *a, b.* H. 455–458. C. & S. 119, 1–9.

30. Which is used in a *particular negation* and which in a *general?*
A. & G. 202, *b*.   H. 455, 456.   C. & S. 119, 3, 5.

31. What kind of a pronoun is *ipse?*
A. & G. 100.   H. 452, 1, 2, 3, 4, 5, 6, 7.   C. & S. 118, 1, 2.

32. What distinction is made between *se* and *ipse?*
A. & G. 102, *e*, note.   H. 449, 1, 1).   C. & S. 117, 1–5, 118, 1, 2.

33. What words are sometimes used as *Reciprocal Pronouns ?*
A. & G. 203, *a, b, c.*   H. 459.   C. & S. 119, 9, *a–c.*

34. Describe the *correlative uses of pronouns.*
A. & G. 106.   H. 191.   C. & S. 63, 1.

ADJECTIVES.

1. What ending has the *Feminine form* of the *First and Second Declension?*   A. & G. 81.   H. 147, 148.   C. & S. 39.

2. What is peculiar in the declension of *miser?*
A. & G. 82.   H. 150, N. 1).   C. & S. 39, 21, 2.

3. What adjectives are declined like *miser*, and what is the difference between the declension of *miser* and *niger ?*
A. & G. 82, *b*.   H. 150, N. 1).   C. & S. 39, 21, 2, 23, 1.

4. What adjectives are declined like *niger ?*
A. & G. 82, *c*.   H. 150, N.   C. & S. 39, 21, 2, 23, 1.

5. What is peculiar in the declension of *totus*, and what are the *nine adjectives* of this class? What is the quantity of *i* in the *Genitive Singular* of each?   A. & G. 83.   H. 151, 1.   C. & S. 41.

6. What adjectives belong to the *Third Declension*, and by what name are they called?
A. & G. 84.   H. 152, i., ii., iii.   C. & S. 42, (1), (2), (3).

7. In what adjectives of the *Third Declension* do you find *ia* in the *Nominative Neuter Plural?*
A. & G. 84, *b*, 85.   H. 63.   C. & S. 45, 4, 29, vii.

8. What forms of the *verb* are used as *Adjectives ?*

9. Are *nouns* ever used as *Adjectives ?*   A. & G. 88, *c*.   H. 441, 3.

10. Are *Adjectives* ever used as *nouns ?*
    A. & G. 88, *a*, 188, *a*, *c*. H. 441, 1, 2. C. & S. 113, 7, 8.

11. What is the *Vocative Singular* of *meus ?*
    A. & G. 81, *a*. H. 185, N. 1. C. & S. 23, 3.

12. What is the ending of the *Masculine Genitive Singular* of the
    Nominative ending ius ?   A. & G. 81, *a*.

13. What *Feminine forms* lack a *Masculine Nominative Singular ?*
    A. & G. 82, *d*. H. 159, ii.

14. What is the difference in the two forms of the *Genitive Plural*
    of *celer ?*   A. & G. 84, *c*. C. & S. 42, 1.

15. What is meant by *adjectives of one termination ?*
    A. & G. 85, *a*. H. 155. C. & S. 42, (3), 45.

16. What is the distinction in the use of the forms of the ablative
    singular which end in *i* and *e ?* A. & G. 87, *a*. C. & S. 45, 1.

17. In what adjectives do you find the *Genitive Plural* in *um ?*
    A. & G. 87, *d*. H. 158, 2, 1), 2), 3), 4). C. & S. 45, 3, 4.

18. What signification have the following *adjective endings :* *ŭlus,
    ădes, ensis, ūlus, āris, ternus, ax, eus, ilis, minus, bundus ?*
    A. & G. 164. H. 328–334. C. & S. 104, 1–52.

19. Write the ending signifying, *provided with, quality, passive
    qualities, full of, gentile, son of, diminution.*
    A. & G. 164. H. 328–334. C. & S. 104, 1–52.

20. Form words denoting *parentage* from *Atlas, Tyndaris, Æneas.*
    A. & G. 164, *b*. H. 322. C. & S. 104, 34.

21. Form words with the *diminutive signification* from *puer, homo,
    avus, mulier.*   A. & G. 164, *a*. H. 321. C. & S. 104, 25.

22. Form *adjectives* denoting *material* or *relation* from *rex, patres.*
    A. & G. 164, *g*. H. 330. C. & S. 104, v., 41, 42.

23. Form *adjectives* denoting *full of* or *prone to* from *ira, pisces,
    gloria.*   A. & G. 164, *k*. H. 328. C. & S. 104, v., 43.

24. Form adjectives denoting *quality* or *tendency* from the verbs
    pugno, bibo, noceo. A. & G. 164, *l*. C. & S. 104, iv., 36, 1–4.

25. Form adjectives signifying *passive qualities* from the verbs *frango* and *nasco*.

> A. & G. 164, *m.*   H. 333.   C. & S. 104, iv., 36, 1–4.

26. Other exercises of a similar nature can be given by the teacher with great profit.
In a tabular form, write the significant endings of adjectives.

Comparison of Adjectives.

27. How are *adjectives* regularly *compared?*

> A. & G. 89.   H. 160, 161, 162.   C. & S. 47.

28. What adjectives form their *superlative* by the ending *-rimus?*

> A. & G. 89, *a.*   H. 163, 1.   C. & S. 48.

29. What adjectives form their superlative by the ending *-limus?*

> A. & G. 89, *b.*   H. 163, 2.   C. & S. 48, 1.

30. What adjectives are regularly compared by means of the *adverbs magis* and *maxime?*   A. & G. 89, *d.*   H. 170.   C. & S. 50.

31. How are *participles* compared when used as *adjectives?*

> A. & G. 89, *e.*

32. Compare in full the irregular adjectives *bonus, malus, magnus, parvus, multus, nequam, frugalior, dexter.*

> A. & G. 90.   H. 165, N. 2.   C. & S. 49, 1.

33. Give the *full comparison* of the comparatives *citerior, interior, prior, propior, ulterior.*   A. & G. 91.   H. 166.   C. & S. 49, 1.

34. Compare *exterus, inferus, posterus, superus.*

> A. & G. 91, *a.*   H. 163, 3.   C. & S. 49, 1.

35. Compare *juvenis* and *senex.*

> A. & G. 91, *b.*   H. 168, 4.   C. & S. 49, 1.

36. What peculiar significations have certain *comparatives* and *superlatives?*

> A. & G. 93, *a, b, c, d, e, f,* 192, 193.   H. 458, 1, 2, 444, 1, 2, 3, 440, N. 1, N. 2.   C. & S. 53, 1–6, 113, 10.

37. What are the classes of *numeral adjectives?*

> A. & G. 94, 95.   H. 172, 1, 2, 3.   C. & S. 54, 1, 2, 3.

38. What *numeral adjectives* are *declined?*
A. & G, 94, *a, b, c, d, e.*   H. 175, 176, 177, 178, 179.   C. & S. 55, 3.

39. What is the rule for the *agreement of an adjective?*
A. & G. 186.   H. 438.   C. & S. 113, 1.

40. When an *adjective is used with several nouns* in what *number* is the adjective?   A. & G. 186, *d.*   H. 439.   C. & S. 113, 3.

41. When an *adjective is used with several nouns of different gender*, with which does it agree?
A. & G. 187, *b, c.*   H. 439, 1, 2, 3, 4.   C. & S. 113, 3.

42. What peculiar uses has the *Neuter form of the Adjective?*
A. & G. 189, *a, b, c, d.*   H. 439, 2, N.
C. & S. 113, 3, N. 1, N. 2, 4, 5, 8.

43. Instead of what case is the *Possessive Adjective* sometimes used?
A. & G. 217, *a.*   H. 395, N. 2.   C. & S. 133, N. 3, 116, 10.

44. Of what *adjectives* is the *Genitive used to express indefinite value?*
A. & G. 215, *c.*   H. 404, N. 1, foot-note 2.   C. & S. 146, 1, *a.*

45. What common use has the *Neuter Accusative of the Adjective?*
A. & G. 240, *a.*   H. 375, 378.   C. & S. 124, N. 1.

46. With *what case following* may *cardinal numbers* sometimes be used?
A. & G. 216, *c.*   H. 397, 3, N. 3.   C. & S. 133, 4, notes 4 and 5.

47. What case follows the *comparative degree when quam is omitted?*
A. & G. 247.   H. 417.   C. & S. 174.

48. When is the *Genitive*, and when the *Dative*, used with *similis?*
A. & G. 234, *d.*   H. 391, i., ii. 4, foot-notes 1 and 3. C. & S. 162, 4.

49. What adjectives regularly govern the *Genitive* and what the *Dative* in the following word?
A. & G. 218–234.   H. 391, i., 399, i. 1, 2, 3, ii.
C. & S. 136, 1, 2, 3, 4, 5, 6, 7, 162, 1, 2, 3, 4, 5, 6, 7.

50. What is the *normal position of the adjective* in a sentence?
A. & G. 343, *c.*   H. 565.   C. & S. 259, 1, 9.

51. How is *plus* declined?
A. & G. 86.   H. 165, N. 1.   C. & S. 44, 2.

52. Explain the uses of *primus, primum, primo.*
A. & G. 151, *d.*   H. 554, i. 6, N. 2.   C. & S. 113, 6, notes 1 and 2.

ADVERBS.

1. How are *adverbs* formed from *adjectives of the First and Second Declension?*
A. & G. 81, *b.*   H. 304.   C. & S. 99, 1, *a.*

2. How are *adverbs* formed from *adjectives of the Third Declension?*   A. & G. 84, *d.*   H. 304.   C. & S. 99, 1, *b.*

3. What *cases of the adjective* are used as *adverbs?*
A. & G. 88, *d.*   H. 304, i. 1, 2, 3, 4, ii. 1, 2, 3, iii. 1, 2.   C. & S. 99, 1, *c.*

4. How are *adverbs compared?*
A. & G. 92.   H. 306, 1, 2, 3, 4, 5, 6.   C. & S. 52.

5. Explain the uses of *numeral adverbs.*
A. & G. 96.   H. 181.   C. & S. 54, 3, 55, 5, 8, 9.

6. Mention and explain the *origin* of some of the *adverbs of place, time, degree, or cause.*
A. & G. 149.   H. 305, i., ii., iii., iv., v.   C. & S. 99, 2, 3.

7. What *adverbs,* and with what case following, are used as *prepositions?*   A. & G. 207, *b.*   H. 398, 5, 437, 1, 2, 3.
C. & S. 131, 2, 133, 7, 1, 162, 6.

8. What is the *normal position of the adverb* in a sentence?
A. & G. 343.   H. 567.   C. & S. 259, 7.

9. What *demonstrative pronoun* is often used adverbially?
A. & G. 195, *e.*   H. 451, 3.   C. & S. 116, 7.

PREPOSITIONS.

1. What is the *common use* of *prepositions?*
A. & G. 152.   H. 307.   C. & S. 101.

2. What *prepositions* are used with the *Accusative?*
A. & G. 152, *a.*   H. 433.   C. & S. 131, 1.

3. What *prepositions* are used with the *Ablative?*
A. & G. 152, *b.*   H. 434.   C. & S. 186.

4. What *prepositions* sometimes are used with the *Accusative* and sometimes with the *Ablative?*
A. & G. 152, *c.*   H. 435.   C. & S. 131, 3, 4.

5. What is the *distinction* in the use of the *prepositions* in Question 4? A. & G. 152, *c*, 260, *c*, *d*. H. 435, 1. C. & S. 131, 3, 4.

6. What *prepositions compounded with verbs* govern the *Dative?*
A. & G. 228, 229. H. 386. C. & S. 154.

7. State the peculiar uses of *ad* with the *Accusative*.
A. & G. 259, *f*, 318, 259, *b*. H. 433, i., 408, i. 3, 446, N. 4, 542, foot-note 5, 542, iii. N. 2. C. & S. 115, 2, 142, 4, 183, 6, *a*, 252, 11, 12.

8. What are the *uses of prepositions* in expressing *place?*
A. & G. 229, *a*, 259, *f*. H. 380, i., ii. 1, 2, 1), 2), 3, 412, i., ii., 425, i., ii., 426, 1, 2, 427, i., ii., iii., 428, i., ii., iii. C. & S. 131, 3. 182, 2. 183, 1, 2, 5, 6, *a*, *b*, 184.

9. What construction follows compounds of *ab*, *de*, *ex*, when used figuratively? A. & G. 243, *b*. H. 434, N. 1. C. & S. 151.

10. In expressions of *source* or *material*, what is the use of *prepositions?*
A. & G. 244, *a*, also re. H. 415, i., ii., iii. C. & S. 172, 178, 1, 2, 3.

11. In expressions of *cause*, what is the use of the *preposition?*
A. & G. 245, also *b*. H. 416, i. 1), 2). C. & S. 166.

12. What *preposition* is used with the *Voluntary Agent?*
A. & G. 246, also *b*. H. 388, 2, 415, 1. C. & S. 173, 1, 2.

13. When does the *Ablative of manner* require the use of *cum?*
A. & G. 248, re. H. 419, iii. N. 1. C. & S. 166, 1, 2, 3.

14. When does the *Ablative of accompaniment* require, and when omit *cum?*
A. & G. 248, *a*. H. 419, i. also 1, 1), 2). C. & S. 166, 5.

15. What *preposition* is frequently used with *words of contention?*
A. & G. 248, *b*. H. 419, 1, 2). C. & S. 166, 5.

16. What *preposition* is frequently used with *verbs of exchanging*, etc.? A. & G. 252, *c*. H. 422, N. 2. C. & S. 179, 3.

17. What is the use of *prepositions* in *expressions of time?*
A. & G. 256, *a*. H. 379, 1, 429, 1, 2. C. & S. 129, 1, 2, 3, 185, 10, 4.

18. What *adverbs* are frequently used as *prepositions* and with what *cases?* A. & G. 261, *a, b, c.* H. 398, 5, 437, 1, 2, 3. C. & S. 131, 2, 133, 7, 1, 162, 6.

19. What is the *regular position of a preposition* in a sentence? A. & G. 345, *a.* H. 569, ii. C. & S. 259, 3, 4.

20. What *prepositions* sometimes follow their *nouns?* A. & G. 263, note. H. 569, ii. C. & S. 259, 5, 131, 5.

21. With what *case* is *instar* used? A. & G. 214, *g.* H. 398, 4. C. & S. 133, 7.

22. With what *case* is *ergo* used? A. & G. 214, *g.* H. 398, 5. C. & S. 133, 7.

CONJUNCTIONS AND INTERJECTIONS.

1. Define and illustrate *conjunctions.* A. & G. 25, *h.* H. 309, 310, 311. C. & S. 100, i. 1, 2, 3, 4, 5, 6; ii. 1, 2, 3, 4, 5, 6, 7.

2. What *adverbs* are sometimes used as *conjunctions?* A. & G. 107. H. 555, ii. 1. C. & S. 63, 2.

3. How are *conjunctions* supposed to have originated? A. & G. 154. C. & S. 98.

4. Classify *conjunctions* and give examples in English and Latin of each class. A. & G. 154, *a, b,* 155, *A, B, C, D, E, F, G, H.* H. 309, 310, 311. C. & S. 100, i. 1, 2, 3, 4, 5, 6, ii. 1, 2, 3, 4, 5, 6, 7.

5. Explain the difference between the uses of the conjunctions *et, que,* and *atque.* A. & G. 156, *a.* H. 554, i. 2.

6. State the signification of the *conjunctions sed* and *verum, at* and *tamen, Quod si, vere* and *autem.* A. & G. 156, *b.* H. 554, iii. 2.

7. State the use of *vel;* also *vel minimus.* A. & G. 156, *c.* H. 554, ii. 2. C. & S. 257, 4.

8. Explain the difference in the use of *Nam, enim,* and *etenim.* A. & G. 156, *d.* H. 554, v. 1, 2, 3.

9. Explain the difference in the use of *Quia, quod, quoniam.*
A. & G. 156, *f.*

10. What is the force of *et* in translation when connecting consecutive clauses? A. & G. 156, *h.* H. 554, i. 5. C. & S. 257, 6.

11. What is the position of *enim, vero, autem,* in a sentence?
A. & G. 156, *k.* H. 569, iii. C. & S. 259, 20.

12. Explain the use of *Copulative and Disjunctive Conjunctions.*
A. & G. 208. H. 554, i., ii., 310, 1, 2. C. & S. 100, i. 1, 2.

13. Explain the use and force of *negative particles.*
A. & G. 209, *a, b, c, d, e.* H. 552, 1, 2, 3, 553, 1, 2.
C. & S. 256, 1, 2, 3, 4.

14 Mention the *Common Interjections* and their uses.
A. & G. 155. H. 312, 1, 2, 3, 4, 5, 6, 556, 557.
C. & S. 102, i. 1, 2, 2, 1, 2, 3.

PHRASES AND CLAUSES.

1. What is a *phrase?* A. & G. 179.

2. What are the *classes of phrases,* and how is each used?
A. & G. 179.

3. What is a *clause?* A. & G. 180.

4. Mention the *classes of clauses.*
A. & G. 180, *a, b, c, d, e, f.* H. 348, N. 2. C. & S. 107, 3.

5. Express in a tabular form the syntax of *Dependent clauses.*
A. & G. 316–342. H. 371, iv., 431, N. 1, 445, 7, 498, 499, 503, 1, N. 1, 513, 514, 518, 524. C. & S. 236, 206, 207, 187, 5.

6. State and explain the uses of *Conditional Relative Clauses.*
A. & G. 316. H. 507, iii. 2. C. & S. 221.

7. Express in a tabular form all the uses of *clauses of purpose.*
A. & G. 317, 318, 331. H. 497, 498, 533, ii., 542, i. N. 2, iii.
N. 2, 544, 2, N. 2, 546, 549, 3. C. & S. 206, 1, 2, 4, 222,
N. 2, 244, 1, 249, 1, 250, 252, 6, 7, 9, 10, 12, 253, N.

8. Express in a tabular form the uses of *clauses of result.*
A. & G. 319, 320, *f.* 332. H. 500–505. C. & S. 207, 208, 209.

9. Explain the use of the adjectives *dignus, indignus, idoneus,* and *aptus* with *result clauses.*

A. & G. 320, *f.*   H. 503, ii. 2.   C. & S. 223, 2.

10. Explain the uses of *Causal clauses.*

A. & G. 321, 326.   H. 516, 517.   C. & S. 214, 3, 224, 232.

11. Express in a tabular form the uses of *Temporal clauses.*

A. & G. 323–328.   H. 518–521.   C. & S. 214.

12. Define, illustrate, and classify *Substantive clauses.*

A. & G. 329, 1, 2, 3, 4.   H. 540, i., ii., iii., iv.   C. & S. 208, 209, 212.

13. State the chief uses of *Infinitive clauses.*

A. & G. 330, 272, re.   H. 524, 1, 1), 533, 534, 535, 538, 539.
C. & S. 209, 2, 3, 238–240, 241, 5, 226, 228, 244, 1, 2, 3, 4.

14. State the force and use of a clause with its verb in the *Indicative* introduced by *quod.*

A. & G. 333.   H. 516, i.   C. & S. 232, 233.

15. Explain the uses and force of *Indirect Questions.*

A. & G. 334, 338.   H. 529.   C. & S. 231.

16. Explain the principles of *Indirect Discourse* as affecting its clauses.   A. & G. 336–338.   H. 523–531.   C. & S. 228–230.

Give examples of every case.

SENTENCES.

1. Define the term *sentence* and state the different kinds.

A. & G. 171, *a, b, c, d,* 180.   H. 346, 347, 348, 349, 350, 351.
C. & S. 107, 1, 2, 3.

2. Name the *essential parts.*

A. & G. 172, 173.   H. 346, 356.   C. & S. 107.

3. Is the *subject* necessarily expressed?

A. & G. 174, 175.   H. 368, 2.   C. & S. 108, 2.

4. What is the *position of the subject* with reference to other words in the sentence?   A. & G. 343.   H. 560.   C. & S. 259, 1.

5. Define the terms *Complement, Copula,* and *copulative verbs,* as used in a sentence. A. & G. 176, also *a, b.*   C. & S. 108, 3, 1, 2.

6. What is the *position of the verb* of the predicate?

> A. & G. 343. H. 560. C. & S. 259, 1.

7. How does the position of the *modifier of the subject* differ from that of the modifiers of the verb?

> A. & G. 343. H. 560. C. & S. 259, 1.

8. Define the term *Period or Periodic Sentence* and explain its structure.

> A. & G. 345, N., 346, also *a, b, c, d.* H. 573. C. & S. 263.

DATES; AND NAMES OF PERSONS.

1. Of what did the *Roman day* consist, and how was it divided?

> H. 645, 1, 2. C. & S. 313, 1, 2.

2. How many *days and months* were in the *Roman calendar ?*

> A. & G. N. before 376. H. 641. C. & S. 313, 3.

3. When and what were the *Calends ?*

> A. & G. 376, *a.* H. 642, i. 1. C. & S. 313, 3.

4. When and what were the *Ides ?*

> A. & G. 376, *b.* H. 642, i. 3. C. & S. 313, 3.

5. When and what were the *Nones ?*

> A. & G. 376, *c.* H. 642, i. 2. C. & S. 313, 3.

6. How were the *days of the month* reckoned with reference to these points of time?

> A. & G. 376, *d.* H. 642, ii., iii., 644, i., ii. C. & S. 313, 3, 4, 5.

7. How was the *year stated and reckoned?*

> A. & G. N. before 376. C. & S. 313, 8.

Write in Latin the date of the birth of Cicero.
Write in Latin the date of the birth of Cæsar.
Write in Latin the date of the death of each.

1. How many *names* had each Roman man? A. & G. 80. H. 649.

2. How many *names* had each Roman woman?

> A. & G. 80, *c.* H. 649, 4.

3. What was the *name* designating the *gens* called ?

A. & G. 80, *a*.   H. 649, 331, N. 2.

4. What was the *name* designating the *family* called ?

A. & G. 80, *a*.   H. 649.

5. What was the *name* designating the *person* called?

A. & G. 80, *a*.   H. 649.

6. What was the *agnomen?*   A. & G. 80, *b*.   H. 649, 2.

A Hand-Book of Latin Synonyms.

By EDGAR S. SHUMWAY, A.M., Adjunct Professor (in charge) of Latin, Rutgers College; Principal of the Chautauqua *Academia;* Editor of *Latine.* **Introd. Price, 30 cts.**

1. What Synonyms. These synonyms comprise only those which are used in classical Latin. The number is purposely limited: first, to those whose likeness and difference can be made evident to the student; second, to those which are used frequently enough to make their acquisition of value in vocabulary-building.

2. How classified. Each group of synonyms is headed by that English word which expresses the most general meaning of the group. These groups are then arranged in the alphabetical order of these English list-words, and numbered for ready reference. Within the group each synonym is printed in bold-faced type, and with its definition has a separate paragraph. The most general Latin term is usually placed first in the group. An index of Latin words renders the finding of synonyms for Latin words very easy.

3. Method of treatment. Conciseness has been studied as well as clearness. Especial stress is put on derivations as often giving the readiest clue to differences. Opposites are frequently inserted to make use of other groups which have been already learned. Cross-references indicate groups not far separated in meaning. Throughout the work the needs of two classes have been consulted: first, of the translator of Latin, who should express the proper flavor of the word; secondly (and chiefly), of the writer of Latin, who must exercise great care in his choice of terms. To give still more aid to the Latin writer, frequent cautions have been inserted to help him to the idiom, — to a pure Latinity.

4. In general. The hand-book is of size convenient for the pocket, and in flexible covers. It is designed to meet the needs not only of the college student, but also of the preparatory school. The study of synonyms should begin with the earliest lessons in Latin, and never cease. By no other method can a vocabulary be so speedily and surely mastered, or so great interest aroused. Prepared by a teacher who understands the defects in the ordinary apparatus for the study of Latin in the preparatory school as well as college, and tested not only with pupils but with classes of teachers, this compendium is nothing if not practical.

GINN, HEATH, & CO., Publishers.

A Brief History of Roman Literature.

For Schools and Colleges. Translated and edited from the German edition of Bender by Professors E. P. CROWELL and H. B. RICHARDSON of Amherst College. Square 16mo. 152 pages. Mailing Price, $1.10; Introduction, $1.00.

This work was received with great favor in Germany, and was widely adopted by the secondary schools.

The present translation adapts it to the use of schools and colleges in America, not only by retaining all that is valuable in the German work, but by adding copious references to the best general and special English works on Roman literature.

The table of contents has been greatly enlarged, so as to constitute a complete analysis of the whole, and the chart at the end has been put into better form ; in short, the aim has been to make it a serviceable handbook for students and teachers.

The chief excellence of the work consists in its terse, suggestive, and admirable characterizations of the Roman writers and of their times. It contains just what the student ought to know, and suggests much for the teacher to enlarge upon.

C. S. Harrington, *Prof. of Latin, Wesleyan Univ.:* A very convenient and complete compend for the use of students.

W. A. Packard, *Prof. of Latin, Princeton Coll.:* An excellent compendium, in translating and editing which the editors have done a good service.

Oscar Howes, *Prof. of Latin, Madison Univ.:* It is a valuable little book, supplying a conspicuous want, and rendering possible what was before well-nigh impracticable, the effective class-study of Roman Literature.

Edmund H. Smith, *Prof. of Latin, Hobart Coll., N.Y.:* I desire to speak of it in terms of high commendation. I have no doubt it will prove of great use to college classes.

A. G. Hopkins, *Prof. of Latin, Hamilton Coll.:* It is the only satisfactory manual of the kind for the use of school and college with which I am acquainted.

Geo. O. Holbrooke, *Prof. of Latin in Trinity Coll., Ct.:* It is a book which has been greatly needed in American Colleges, and could not have been better introduced than by Professors Crowell and Richardson.

John Avery, *Prof. of Greek, Bowdoin Coll.:* It seems to me a very useful manual. It has one advantage over Cruttwell's work, that, while reasonably full in its survey of the literature, it is so inexpensive as to be within the reach of college classes.

Geo. E. Jackson, *Prof. of Latin, Washington Univ., St. Louis :* It seems to me the very book for the undergraduate, discriminating, comprehensive, and yet concise and attractive. I shall make trial of it another year.

An Etymology of Latin and Greek.

With a Preliminary Statement of the New System of Indo-European Phonetics, and Suggestions in Regard to the Study of Etymology. By CHARLES S. HALSEY, A.M., Principal of Union Classical Institute, Schenectady, N.Y. 12mo. Cloth. 272 pages. Mailing Price, $1.25. Introduction, $1.12.

The following are the prominent features of the work : —

1. It presents the subject in a systematic form. The general principles and laws of the science are first clearly stated and illustrated ; then the words are treated in their etymological order. This produces a result far better than can be obtained from the mere study of detached words scattered irregularly through a lexicon.

2. It gives a new and simple plan, presenting side by side for each group of related words the form of the root in Indo-European, Sanskrit, Greek, and Latin, with the meaning of the root. Following these roots are the most practical Greek words and the most practical Latin words, with their meanings. This furnishes a valuable stock of words associated by the natural bond of their common derivation, each language, too, throwing light upon the other.

3. It presents within moderate compass the results of the latest investigations of the highest authorities, omitting doubtful etymologies, and is thus at once rigidly scientific and thoroughly practical.

4. It gives great prominence to the derivation of English words, supplying to a large degree the place of an English etymology.

5. Being furnished with a complete index for every root and word treated, it can be conveniently used as a work of reference.

6. It presents the entire subject in a form thoroughly adapted to school use in classes. The study of Etymology, as here presented, may begin with the very outset of the study of Latin, and be continued through the entire course of classical study. It may be pursued with a separate recitation, or in brief portions, in connection with the recitations from the Greek and Latin authors.

7. The present work is the first school-book to set forth in the English language the principles and the application of the new system of I.-E. Phonetics. This it does in full, and in a practical and intelligible form. This work may be used without confusion in connection with any grammar or lexicon ; and it supplies thoroughly what they may lack in the important department of Etymology.

Madvig's Latin Grammar.

Carefully revised by THOMAS A. THACHER, Professor of Latin, Yale College. 12mo. Half morocco. 515 pages. Mailing Price, $2.50; Introduction, $2.25.

Whatever may be the preferences for one or another modern Latin Grammar, the scholars of the country agree in placing *Madvig's Latin Grammar* as the highest authority for reference yet issued.

H. S. Frieze, *Prof. of Latin, Univ. of Mich.:* As a grammar for reference, and for the cultivation of thorough scholarship in Latin, I think it unequalled.

J. B. Greenough, *Prof. of Latin, Harvard Coll.:* A book that all students who wish to go beyond the rudiments of Latin ought to have and study.

Charles Short, *Prof. of Latin, Columbia Coll.:* Prof. Madvig is known as one of the greatest of living classical scholars, — great in Greek as well as in Latin. We congratulate American teachers that they can now procure this valuable work in an enlarged and improved state, and that at one-third the English price.

B. L. Cilley, *Prof. of Greek, Phillips Exeter Acad.:* It is the best grammar for reference with which I am ac-quainted. No *teacher* of Latin should be without it.

The Nation: May justly be pro-nounced the most important aid to Latin scholarship which our community has for a long time received. We should decidedly prefer Madvig to Zumpt for college use. Madvig adds to comprehensiveness and accuracy a far superior power of generalization; or, at any rate, taking up the analysis of the usages of the language where Zumpt left it, he has carried it still further. At the same time, this more philosophical treatment is not *à priori* or over-theoretical: the generalizations are purely the result of the observation of facts, not of preconceived theories, so that the grammar is in the main just what a grammar should be, — a well-digested analysis of actual facts and usages.

The Latin Verb.

Illustrated by the Sanskrit. By C. H. PARKHURST, formerly of Williston Seminary. 12mo. Cloth. 55 pages. Mailing Price, 40 cts.; Introduction, 35 cts.

The *immediate* aim of this treatise is to familiarize the student with the earlier and later forms of the Latin verb, and the method by which the latter has been corrupted from the former. The *immediate* aim is to introduce the pupil to the study of Comparative Grammar.

Ginn & Heath's Classical Atlas.

By A. KEITH JOHNSTON, LL.D., F.R.G.S., aided by W. E. GLADSTONE, Prime Minister of England. Contains also a **Geography of the Ancient World,** prepared by W. F. ALLEN of the Univ. of Wisconsin. Bound in full cloth, with guards, similar to Long's Classical Atlas (7½ X 12 inches). Mailing price, $2.30; Introduction, $2.00.

We would call special attention to the binding of the cloth edition. It is mounted on guards, the binding thus costing about twice as much as that of the English edition, and yet we do not increase the price to the purchaser. As a book of this kind is in constant use, the stronger binding very much enhances its value.

Comprising in Twenty-three Plates, Colored Maps and Plans of all the important countries and localities referred to by Classical Authors. Embodies the results of the most recent investigations. Has a full **Index of Places,** in which the proper quantities of the syllables are marked by T. HARVEY and E. WORSLEY, M.M.A., Oxon, Classical Masters in Edinburgh Academy. Also containing ALLEN'S **Geography of the Ancient World,** which is designed to bring the leading epochs and events of ancient history into connection with the geography of the ancient world. Brief suggestions to teachers are added, to assist in the work of the class-room.

"It has the special attraction of Mr. Gladstone's coöperation, who not only placed at the editor's disposal the illustrations to his work on Homer, but enhanced the favor by revising the proof-sheets of the plates and text, as adapted for this Atlas."—*Spectator.*

CONTENTS.

Map.
1. Plan of Rome, and Illustrations of Classical Sites.
2. The World as known to the Ancients.
3. Map of the outer Geography of the Odyssey.
4. Orbis Terrarum (et Orb. Homeri, Herodoti, Democriti, Straboris, Ptolemæi).
5. Hispania.
6. Gallia.
7. Insulæ Britanicæ (et Brit. Strabonis, Brit. Ptolemæi, etc.).
8. Germania, Vindelicia, Rhætia, et Noricum.
9. Pannonia, Dacia, Illyricum, Mœsia, Macedonia, et Thracia.
10. Italia Superior et Corsica.
11. Italia Inferior, Sicilia, et Sardinia (et Campania, Syracusæ, Roma).

12. Imperium Romanum (et Imp. Rom. Orient. et Occid.).
13. Græcia (et Athenæ, Marathon, Thermopylæ).
14. Peloponnesus, Attica, Bœotia, Phocis, Ætolia, et Acarnania.
15. Græcia a Bello Peloponnesiaco, usque ad Philippum II. (et Mantinea, Leuctra, Platæa).
16. Asia Minor (et Campus Trojæ, Bosporos, Troas, Ionia, etc.).
17. Syria et Palestina (et Hierosolyma, etc.).
18. Armenia, Mesopotamia, Babylonia, Assyria (et Iter Xenophontis).
19. Regnum Alexandri Magni (et Granicus, Issus, Arbela).
20. Persia et India (et India Ptolemæi).
21. Ægyptus, Arabia, et Æthiopia (et Ægyptus Inferior).
22. Africa (et Carthago, Alexandria, Numidia et Africa Propria).
23. Europe, showing the general direction of the Barbarian Inroads during the Decline and Fall of the Roman Empire.

     Index.

     Allen's Geography of the Ancient World.

Used at **Eton, Harrow, Rugby,** and other Prominent English Preparatory Schools and Academies. Also used and recommended by such Colleges and Preparatory Schools as : —

Harvard,	**Trinity, Conn.,**	**Hillsdale,**
Yale,	**Trinity, N.C.,**	**Dickinson,**
Lafayette,	**N. W. University,**	**Wesleyan, Conn.,**
Rutgers,	**Wesleyan, Ill.,**	**Princeton,**
Oberlin,	**Lake Forest,**	**Bates,**
Marietta,	**Wisconsin,**	**Grinnell,**
Worcester Univ.,	**Beloit,**	**Colby,**
Ohio Wesleyan,	**Lawrence, Wis.,**	**Kentucky Univ.,**
Hiram,	**Olivet,**	**Vanderbilt.**
Phillips Exeter Academy,	**Phillips Andover Academy,**	
Williston Seminary,	**Boston Latin Schools, etc.**	

W. W. Goodwin, *Prof. of Greek, Harvard Univ.:* It is a most beautiful and highly useful work, and I am glad to see what used to be an expensive luxury brought within the means of all students of the classics. (*Dec. 2, 1880.*)

Elisha Jones, *Asst. Prof. of Latin, Univ. of Mich.:* From my cursory acquaintance I have recommended it to our teachers. The map of the Homeric Geography is a feature not contained in either of my other atlases, and will aid Homeric students greatly.

Tracy Peck, *Prof. of Latin, Yale Coll.:* I have heretofore known the Atlas sufficiently well to feel justified in recommending it to inquiring students. (*May 9, 1881.*)

S. R. Winans, *Tutor in Greek, Princeton Coll., N.J.:* It is superb: nothing to criticise, and everything to commend. Every student of the classics needs something of the sort, and this is by all odds the best of its kind. (*Oct. 4, 1880.*)